Golf's Great Twin Miracles
BALLYLIFFIN

How such a tiny and remote community as Ballyliffin has come to possess two of
the world's finest golf links is the stuff of legend. Some would say it is the
stuff of miracles. The Old Links, it was opened in 1973, and the
new Glashedy Links stand side by side as contrasting but
equally lovely and enthralling challenges to players of
all levels of expertise. Here, the visiting golfer is
warmly welcomed and treated as family.
Ballyliffin is now one of the world's great golf resorts with every member
of the community speaking about the game and most of them
employed, or with family members employed, in the game.
This is the story of Ballyliffin's rise into the elite of world golf destinations.

PAT RUDDY

With photography by Pat Ruddy

The par-4 third hole brings play into the high dunes.

First published in 2014
by the

RUDDY GOLF LIBRARY

The European Club
Brittas Bay, County Wicklow, Ireland
info@theeuropeanclub.com

For those club members who worked so hard on the Development Committee of Glashedy Links
including Patsy Doherty, Packie Farren, Barry Kearney, P.J. McDaid, Brian Harkin,
John McGeoghegan, Karl O'Doherty and Cormac McDonough.

A special thought for my late friend, partner and hero Tom Craddock with whom I shared the joys of so many long
trips to Donegal and, after the day's work, monster dinners and golf talk into the night in the Strand Hotel.

ISBN 978-0-9556049-3-5

Printed in Hong Kong.

The game is on. Looking back from the first green on Glashedy.

Preface

My first contact with Ballyliffin was in the 1960s when my old friend and hero Joe Masterson moved there from Sligo and started to pester me to give publicity to this amazing golf club that he had discovered in the furthest northwest corner of Ireland. "It is the best, it is unimaginable, you must come and see it for yourself but meantime you must write about it!", he urged me week after week. I obeyed him. I trusted Joe.

He was one of those larger than life men who played football for club and county, ran the local amateur drama festival, played tennis, boxed, and took to golf with a half-crazed relish. So, I trusted Joe and I wrote about Ballyliffin and their open weeks and their links in my golf columns in the Dublin "Evening Herald".

But, to my shame, I never got around to going there during Joe's lifetime. The troubles in Northern Ireland caused the place to seem isolated from Dublin. So Joe died without a reunion and Ballyliffin slipped off one's radar.

Eventually, in 1992, Ballyliffin came back into my life with a telephone call from the club asking whether I would be interested in looking at their links with a view to improving the bunkering and perhaps suggest some other possible improvements. It was still a long way to Ballyliffin and I was afraid that a small country club might not like the sound of the fees one would require and so we agreed to have our first meeting halfway between us in a hotel in Monaghan. Six of them came and nobody offered to buy a cup of tea! I was right!

But I was wrong. I had them wrong. Barry Kearney was their tough talker. He turned-out to be a man with a heart of gold but his job that night was to test me out. When I named a fee structure he swooned. He moaned. He groaned. But he and they listened to my proposals and we agreed on a visit to Ballyliffin. My late pal and partner Tom Craddock and I would visit them within a few weeks.

When we got to Ballyliffin and I saw that the club had almost 400-acres of beautiful dunesland it was my turn to swoon. What a great place. What a great opportunity to build another great golf links. But we had to move fast because of upcoming restrictive planning laws. "Forget about bunkering the links you have," I urged, "let's build a world beating second links. We can get back to bunkering your existing links later."

I was crazy. I would have been run out of town for such a suggestion almost anywhere else. How could a small rural golf club possibly build a second golf links? Well, they proved just as crazy and visionary as myself and we set to work to see what could be done. The result is nothing short of a golfing miracle.

PAT RUDDY

Brittas Bay, November 2014

Things look more serious from Glashedy's second tee.

The Glashedy starts to climb towards the plateau at the second green.

INDOMITABLE IRISH SPIRIT
Where there is a dream there is a pathway.

The only way to understand how a tiny village in the far north of Donegal came to possess two of the finest golf links on the planet is through an understanding of the Irish manner of doing things.

The seed of an idea is sown. This grows into a dream. And shure and begorrah it gets done!

Never mind that the golfers don't own land. No heed that they do not have the money to undertake the project. Not a bother that there are not enough golfers to sustain a club. The spirit of the Irish will win the day.

The modern golfer may find it difficult to understand how golf began from simple origins. Difficult to grasp how so many great golf clubs began modestly and developed their facilities over decades. It was so different back then from the modern formula of spending millions to develop an instantly matured golf course with luxury clubhouse and, maybe, an hotel and some luxury homes.

Portrush began life over rough dunesland with a small thatched hut, not more than four or five steps square, as the first clubhouse.

The golfers at Newcastle, now Royal County Down, started life travelling by train from Belfast and using a waiting-room at the local railway station as their first clubhouse. They played cards in a specially reserved carriage on the train on the way down each saturday, played golf over rugged dunes all day, and played cards again on the way home. All they wanted was a day away from the cares of the city with their friends.

In Dublin the golfers played over a makeshift course on public ground in the Phoenix Park and persevered despite frequent destruction of their greens by the charging cavalry out for training runs from the local barracks! So they transferred to the linksland at Dollymount and have come to be known as The Royal Dublin Golf Club.

It was the same with the game's pioneers in America where in 1888 a chap named John Reid gathered some friends to play over a three-hole course in Yonkers. They became known as the Apple Tree Gang because they hung their coats off an apple tree while playing. From such modest beginnings they went on to become the St. Andrews Golf Club and to stage the first U.S. "Open" and to be one of the founding group of the United States Golf Association.

Clubhouses were the exception rather than the rule in early Scottish golf, too. Most often they retired to a local inn for drink and food and song after the golf and there is the famous story of one such party getting out of hand. Too much claret had been imbibed and somehow a waiter was thrown out of the window of the upstairs dining room.

14

The thrill of playing from a high tee on Glashedy's third hole.

When the inn owner enquired as to what should be done concerning the waiter he was told: "Put him on the bill!"

Since those early days golf has ridden a roller-coaster ride of boom and recession, war and peace, but the overall trend has been upward and forward.

So it has been at Ballyliffin where golf was first played in the 1920s but it took until 1947 to see a golf club take formal shape. Land for nine holes was leased near the village. There was no question of affording a clubhouse other than a small nissen hut made of corrugated steel and the main club functions were held in the Strand Hotel.

The solitary greenkeeper was helped by volunteers from amongst the members who formed the habit of bringing their own lawnmowers to cut a few greens or tees before going out to play! This was the age of the volunteer across the land, except for the big city clubs, and the result was often an uneven quality of greens as some men mowed their designated patches while others did not and, of course, not all mowers were set to the same height of cut or properly sharpened. But the game went on and gave much enjoyment everywhere.

It was not until the late 1960s, faced with a non-renewal of their lease, that the Ballyliffin club sought a permanent home in the linksland further out from town. Martin Hopkins, who was familiar with all the lands in the area through his role as an agricultural advisor, identified the potential of the linksland for golf and a new era dawned.

The lands were held in commonage and it took sometime for the club to succeed in buying almost 400-acres as several shareholders had to agree to sell their interest in the property. Work started in 1970 on the creation of what is now known as The Old Course and the full 18-holes were in play by 1973. It had been designed by Eddie Hackett who paid many visits, some visits were made by the English architects Charles Lawrie & Frank Pennink, and much credit must go to Martin Hopkins who contributed many design touches while proving a master on the agronomy side of things. Now that the club owned its own property and the links was gaining recognition as one of the best in Ireland the membership started to grow rapidly to the point that Ballyliffin was ready for the amazing events of the 1990s.

THE GLASHEDY LINKS IS CONCEIVED

It was in 1992 that the call came. Would I be interested in advising the club on a revision of bunkering and on other possible improvements on the links? After a preliminary meeting in Monaghan (see story in the Preface) it was agreed that my friend and golf design partner of the time Tom Craddock and I would go to Ballyliffin. What followed was most unexpected and in the realms of a miracle.

On seeing that the club had about 400-acres of dunesland I went into mental superdrive. "Forget new bunkers for your links right now," I advised. "We should set about building a world class second links and it is urgent that we should do so."

Timing is everything in this life. I had just opened my own golf links at The European Club at Brittas Bay and I had learned a great deal in the process and not just about growing grass on sand. I had learned how to qualify, along with

places like The K-Club, The Old Head, Doonbeg, Adare and Mount Juliet amongst others, for a government grant. I knew that environmental labels were being placed on linksland and that the planning laws were about to be changed and make the creation of new golf links almost impossible.

Perhaps I am unusual as a golf course designer. I have always taken an holistic approach to the job. I see it as part of my job not just to deliver a fine course but to help create a project that will succeed for decades to come.

The Ballyliffin men listened as I told them to get to Dublin and see how, at that very moment, red lines were being drawn around their land by conservationists. Their lands could be frozen from development. It was now or maybe never if a new links was to happen as the planning laws for golf were about to be toughened as well. My call to arms got a positive response but there were questions. For example, how could it be done financially?

They listened as I told them that I thought they might get a substantial tourism grant. Ireland had a problem with the provision of golf holidays up to the 1990s insofar as all the better courses were owned by members' clubs who were not welcoming of visitors at weekends when the main club events were taking place. So Ireland could sell only 5-day golf weeks! For this reason it was decided to grant aid new golf developments catering to tourist golfers all week.

Members' clubs were generally unable to qualify for these grants because of the great demands for member play at weekends. But I calculated that a second links at Ballyliffin would leave the club with surplus times to devote to visiting players and that they might qualify for a grant on that basis if they formed a limited company to develop and own the new links and enter legal agreements, as a separate "legal person", with the tourism bodies.

The new company, the "new legal person", could deliver on tourism and the members' interests would be protected as they would own and control the company 100%.

They got active politically. They got the best consultancy advice. They formed a company. They went at it and got a grant of £315,000 which was a huge sum of money at that time and it was a massive boost to a club which had never gained any type of grant previously! Now the game was on. Nothing could stop the inevitable now.

Plans had to be refined. The approval of the members had to be won. But the beauty of the land, the beauty of the timing for grant aid, and my argument that they could soon own two great links instead of one - and have both paid for and, more important, paying their own way so that golf would not become a financial burden for the members - swept events inexorably in the direction of a golfing miracle.

There were those who worried, of course. A long and vital debate took place at an Extraordinary General Meeting in the clubhouse on December 13, 1992 at which I stressed that the members would always have control, and that the members would have two great links instead of one, and that the members would have total access to both links and that the greenfee income I would expect the club to earn from visitors would stabilise membership fees rather than increase them.

The members accepted these arguments and The Twin Miracle of Twin Links at Ballyliffin was set to become reality.

18

Deep pot bunkers await at the green at Glashedy's par-3 fifth hole.

Glashedy Rock comes into view behind the fourth green.

A LOVELY GIANT REVEALED
The dunesland is awakened to golf.

The lovely thing about dunesland is that it is alive with golfing possibilities. Green sites abound. Partial fairways are clear to view along prairies of waving marram grass and through weaving valleys and the ocean vistas are captivating. But it can be bewildering until a plan, a route plan, has been devised.

A hotch potch approach will not do. The lure of a particularly seductive greensite must not lead the designer into a false position such as requiring the golfer to play blindly into the rising or setting sun; or making the walk to the next tee excessively long or unpleasantly steep (especially in Ireland where golf has always been a walking game).

There is much to routing and it is a discipline in which I have revelled ever since taking to geometry with relish in my teens not knowing that it would be so useful in later life and that I would be engaged forever with right and obtuse angles; with isosceles and equilateral triangles; with parallel lines; and with area, volume and distance.

A good route plan will marry geometry with art and an appreciation for beautiful natural forms, hues and textures to maximise the golfing potential of a property and produce a pleasantly walkable course with a carefully orchestrated balance of holes of varying lengths, character and direction. Most modern designs require that the golfer comes back to the clubhouse at green nine. Big decisions are required to get it all synchronised.

It fell to me to devise the route plan for what was to become the Glashedy Links at Ballyliffin and it quickly appeared that a lovely giant golf links was available. There were three dominant factors to take into account: (i) The huge scale of the property; (ii) The fact that an existing links fairly wrapped itself around the clubhouse making it necessary to change some holes to allow the new links get out to open lands twice and back twice; and (iii) The presence of a really massive, exposed sand dune out at the far end of the existing links with much of our available lands located on a lovely isolated plateau behind it and helpfully accessible by easy slopes at the seaward and inland ends.

Tampering with the existing Old Links was contentious and understandably so as it was, and is, very beautiful and good. But it had to be done to allow the Glashedy Links to function and great care was taken to replace any hole that was removed with an even nicer and better one.

The Glashedy plan provided for both the front-nine and back-nine to fairly race out to either end of the big exposed dune and up behind it for a few holes before tumbling back over it and home to the clubhouse. This arrangement allows for

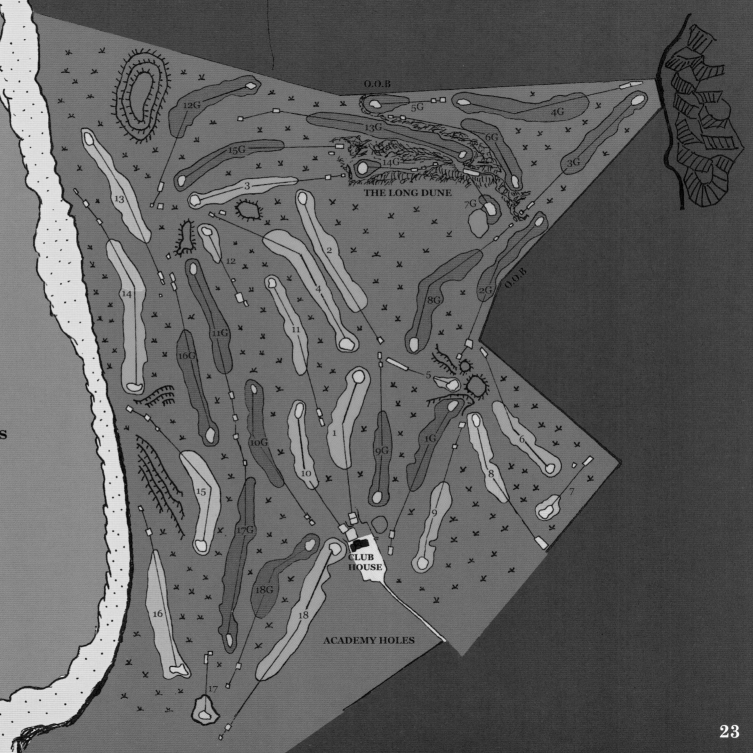

POLLAN
BAY

BALLYLIFFIN
**Outline of the links layout
showing the Glashedy Links
and other design elements
completed by
Craddock & Ruddy.**

Glashedy Links   =   ●

Old Links elements
by C & R =   ○

Not to scale.
Route diagram only.

O.O.B

THE LONG DUNE

O.O.B

CLUB
HOUSE

ACADEMY HOLES

23

the lovely hidden plateau to be visited twice, for the golfer to be brought on top of the great dune for a double treat of great views and exhilarating wind exposure, for the playing in opposite directions of two lovely par-3s (the seventh and fourteenth) from the top of the great dune, and for the direction of play to be varied generally by presenting an anti-clockwise vortex effect on the front-nine and a clockwise vortex on the back-nine.

The first three holes march out to the hidden plateau before the links revolves anti-clockwise on holes four, five, six and seven and then returns to the clubhouse. On the back-nine, holes ten and eleven take two giant strides back out to the other end of the plateau before the the links revolves clockwise on holes twelve, thirteen, fourteen and fifteen and then gallops back to the clubhouse.

The question of clockwise and anti-clockwise movement in a route plan has exercised me for years since noticing that many great links run generally anti-clockwise: St. Andrews Old, Portmarnock, Royal County Down, Royal Portrush, Royal Troon, Royal Dublin, Royal Birkdale, Royal Lytham and many more: and the same is true of so many horse tracks. Could it be that this is because most designers are right-handed and tend to turn right on entering a virgin property to plan a course? Whatever, one has striven since then to vary the circular movements within a course to vary as much as possible the effect of wind and light on the play.

WORRIES ABOUT THE BIG DUNE

Just as there were people concerned about changes to the Old Links there were those, possibly the same people, one never enquired, who did not want anything to be done to change the big dune which did provide a striking backdrop to the links as viewed from the clubhouse. A big white face of sand with whipped edges of marram presented a truly handsome scene.

But there were problems with this dune. First of all it was eroding in the wind and would be gone completely in time if not stabilised. Secondly, the moving sand was blowing over the top of the dune and onto the hidden plateau behind it and burying the new holes, four, five, six, twelve and thirteen which we were seeking to grass in that area!

Stabilisation of the dune was necessary, also, in order to create the twin par-3s coming dramatically off the top of it at holes seven and fourteen. These holes were needed for spatial and routing reasons and for the great drama they would add to the round.

Another debate took place about the difficulty of growing grass on sand in such a northerly location. These worries were put to rest by arranging with Michael Moss that we could visit him at Portstewart Golf Club, just over the waters of Lough Foyle, to see how they had grown grass very successfully on the magnificent new holes designed by club member Des Giffin just a few years earlier.

I had been to Portstewart for a game a year or two before, I like to see what is happening, and I was thrilled by the links and stunned by the rampant growth of the newly planted marram grasses on the great hill to the left of the

The approach to the par-4 sixth on Glashedy.

second fairway! I knew that sight of this would settle all nerves and so it did. Coffee and scones never tasted better than they did when we retreated to the clubhouse to enjoy some Michael Moss hospitality!

Still there were some problems with the big dune. There were concerns about the building of the par-3 fourteenth in a particularly active area of wind erosion. That was settled one cold and wet autumnal night when I went out after dark with two machine men and worked until dawn, chilled to the marrow, doing the necessary shaping. What would happen at daylight? Would there be a stampede of people coming from the clubhouse to put us to death? But it was cold and it was bleak and nobody came and now that hole is regarded as one of the finest par-3s in Irish golf! One other problem existed in the area of the big dune. The land between it and the Old Links had been used for golf a few years earlier but had been abandoned because of flooding. This is why there is a pond beside the green at the par-3 seventh hole. It is in a naturally wet place although the green and immediate surrounds are bone dry. This has become the most photographed hole on the links and appears regularly in golf magazines all over the world!

PERFECTLY BALANCED DESIGN

Golfing one's way up behind the big dune and then emerging on top to play heroic shots down to the par-3 greens at holes seven and fourteen is one of the great experiences in golf. It is like being on a golfing roller coaster with huge anticipation building as the highest point is approached. It is, of course, at its exhilarating best when experienced in a decent breeze from the Atlantic Ocean!

One of the design elements that I like most at Glashedy Links is the total balance of the round. It is a matter of stroke and counter-stroke all the way. The twin vortex effect of the two nines spinning anti-clockwise and then clockwise is really appealing and effective. It is artistically stimulating, one has the mental image of two toy windmills beloved of children with the opening holes on each nine serving as the handles while the holes in the vortexes represent the spinning wheels, and provides for the widest range of wind variations possible over the stretch of holes involved.

There is great balance, too, in the manner in which the two nines start. Both go par-4, par-4, par-4, par-5, par-3 and par-4. This design sequence allows for the game to flow nicely in the early stages with players invited to stride out and get the job done. It also provides an instant challenge to the player from the first tee - Can You Handle Three Decent Par-4 Holes To Start? - before relenting into the 5-3-4 par sequence which offers total variety of shot.

The fact that the last three holes of each nine are played in full sight of the clubhouse presents a lovely "coming home" feel to the game. If one is laden with Stableford points, or within three pars of a great strokeplay score, or holds a lead over an opponent in matchplay this is a classical finishing straight to the winner's enclosure.

There is one final appealing design touch in the way in which the eighteenth holes on the Old Links and the Glashedy Links come racing side-by-side back to the clubhouse in a concelebration of great golf. What fun to have a window seat in a clubhouse looking out over the finishing hole. What bliss to have a seat with a view of two finishing holes!

The par-3 seventh on Glashedy is much photographed.

MARRYING TWO LINKS
Something Old and Something New!

Changes had to be made to the Old Links to allow for the Glashedy Links to get out from and back to the clubhouse with two loops of nine holes. This worried some people who had an understandable attachment to the links as it was. So it was imperative that any changes would be improvements and seen as such from the word go.

It is impossible to explain in words the way in which Ballyliffin Old Links wins the soul of the golfer at first sight. It is so natural. The fairways are so wrinkled. The greens just wink at the player and invite an attack. When the sun is in position to cast shadows the experience becomes virtually extra-terrestrial.

Standing on the first tee is a marvellous experience. The fairway flows away ahead of the player like turbulent ocean waves. It is an effect which is repeated at intervals through a round which is one of the greatest treats in golf.

The job was to change the old links as little as possible and to make sure that any new elements introduced would blend seamlessly with what was untouched. In fact, this brief was exceeded.

On the front-nine, we did not make any changes to holes one, two, three, four, five or six. But we created a new par-3 seventh and a new par-4 eighth hole to allow the old par-3 ninth, which ran alongside the car-park, to be eliminated and so provide space for the first tee on Glashedy Links.

On the back-nine we had nothing to do with holes ten, eleven, twelve, seventeen and eighteen. But we made a lot of improvements besides.

We created a glorious entirely new par-4 thirteenth hole running up a valley that had been an unused flood plain. We raised the entire floor of the plain by a few feet and rippled it strongly but beautifully to match seamlessly with the heaving, contoured character that is the overall hallmark of the Old Links. This has come to be embraced as one of the feature holes.

By going up this previously desolate valley play was brought into position to make a hugely significant improvement to the old thirteenth hole which is now the fourteenth.

The old thirteenth played from a tee near the now twelfth tee on Glashedy Links and the first 160-yards of the fairway often flooded to such a degree that it was impassable. We realigned the first half of the fairway onto higher ground at the oceanside of the valley and placed the tees high on the outer dunes to gain views of the beach and Pollan Bay.

Built on a flood plain. The new thirteenth is a perfect style fit on the Old Links.

We regretted having to eliminate the old par-4 fourteenth as it was a natural beauty running from behind the now fourteenth green on the Old Links to a green close to the now tenth green on Glashedy Links. But this had to happen to let Glashedy's hole eleven get out and holes sixteen and seventeen get back to base. We compensated by creating a smashing new fifteenth hole which is a downhill dog-leg right to a really exciting green. A big improvement on the Old Links.

Our final input on the Old Links was an even more important one at hole sixteen which was a problem hole at the time. It featured a fairway down a valley to a low lying green and both fairway and green flooded to a depth of a few feet most winters. We worked with P.J. McDaid, one of the club's tireless volunteers, on a solution here.

He worked miracles with the drainage but we took no risks and introduced a second and higher level to the fairway on the oceanside and also created an upper deck to the oceanside of the green while leaving the old in place. The hole now has much more variety and many more playing options, is prettier, and is never closed by flooding. It can be said, too, that this is the most Old Links-type hole on the Old Links with by far the most roller-coaster fairway of all!

SMOKIN' JOE'S WAR WITH THE RABBITS.

Life was fun at Ballyliffin when work got underway on creating the Glashedy Links in May 1993. The big story of the time, apart from the new links, centred on the war with the rabbits.

The place was infested with rabbits. They are lovely creatures but with one fatal flaw in their character:- They like to dig. The Old Links was a rabbit heaven with white tails bobbing everywhere and new burrows appearing daily. It is this sort of carry-on that gained them a place in the Rules of Golf (24.2 and 25.1 - abnormal ground conditions).

Things got so bad that the Ballyliffin golfers installed a low chicken-wire fence around every fairway and green, with spring loaded gates that the golfers could push open with their caddy carts, in an effort to keep the rabbits out. But, of course, the varmints just dug tunnels under the fences which had to be taken-up and stone foundations placed under them as an extra line of defence It cost tens of thousands of pounds and didn't work.

Then along came Smokin' Joe Doherty with his tractor and his hoses and the course of the war started to swing in favour of the golfers. Joe would go out for hours and block every rabbit hole he could find around one dune and then connect a hose to the exhaust of the tractor, stick this down one rabbit hole and gas the unfortunate inhabitants.

The war lasted a few years and we revelled in teasing Smokin' Joe when we retreated to the old clubhouse for a cup of tea. Johnny McLaughlin, later of the Strand Hotel, was our host in the clubhouse and he was a master at having a tin of biscuits reserved for our coming and at stirring things up with: "How are things going, Joe?"

My favourite tease was that while Joe was kneeling down at one side of a dune attending to his gas pipe I saw dozens of rabbits emerging from unblocked holes for a hundred yards on the other side of the dune and heading off to new abodes complete with suitcases and odd bits and pieces of rabbit furniture.

Smokin' Joe won in the end and the Old Links and the Glashedy Links have been largely free from rabbits ever since.

The Old Links sixteenth was dramatised by moving to high ground which allowed the introduction of a dramatically heaving fairway.

NO PLACE FOR SLOW PLAY
The Donegal way is to just go and do it.

Once the decision had been made to go ahead and the plans for the Glashedy Links had been accepted things went into high gear. The Donegal way is to just go and do it once a plan is agreed.

Work started on May 7, 1993 and the official opening happened on August 3, 1995. Which has to be record time for shaping, seeding and growing-in a major golf course in such a northern clime. It opened in lovely condition, too.

The fact that a small Development Committee had been put in place to work with us helped a lot. They gave quick decisions when the need arose while reporting back to and getting approvals from the Club Council monthly. This clean line of communication and command is vital in a job as complex as creating a golf course. It becomes very cumbersome if too many people express views every step of the way.

The club appointed Brian Toland as their project manager on site and he proved to be a gem. He had a substantial knowledge of the construction business and, just as important, he was blessed with an even temperament, a will to work and an ability to get the best out of the team of six local men who were engaged full-time along with a rota of part-timers. When Cathal Crawford succeeded Brian Toland he proved to have the same virtues and the job was very harmonious all the way.

It helped, too, that the club agreed a contract with Niall Fanning's construction company from Wicklow. Fanning had worked with us at St. Margaret's Golf & Country Club and at Druids Glen Golf Club and we had developed clear working relationships with the machine men. Here again no time was lost in needless talk as they understood what was required when each phase of work was explained to them and with Tom Craddock and myself on-site directing everything down to the tiniest detail of shaping.

The combination of our extensive design presence, ensuring that things were done right first time, with no time wasted on revisions, and the power-drive approach of the contractor ensured maximum pace on the job. This was a totally new approach to golf course creation in the west of Ireland where things tended to move at a more leisurely pace.

Everyone on the job shared an immense buzz of satisfaction as the great Glashedy Links emerged from the sand dunes in record time. The club powers-that-be clearly liked what they saw emerging because we never received any criticism or request to change anything. We strove to honour that trust and go beyond for a world-class result.

Going for a world-class result has been my philosophy throughout my life in course design. When given a great piece

The dog-leg par-4 eighth on Glashedy turns its back on the great dune!

of land to work with my objective is to create the best golf course possible, suitable for hosting championship play at the highest level, while making it beautiful and very playable by club golfers of all handicaps. I believe that the Glashedy Links is a great success on all fronts and is definitely one of the best golf courses in the world.

Being a golf course designer isn't always a life of wine and roses. Working in golf course design entails a great deal of travel and hotel living. So few jobs happen in one's own back yard! Working at Ballyliffin entailed a good deal of travel to and from Dublin on roads that had not yet been modernised. But the challenge of producing a really great links was exhilarating and all the more pleasurable because I was in partnership with Tom Craddock at that time.

I had been a solo designer since creating my first golf course at Castlecomer in the Irish midlands. It opened in 1972. Things were quiet in Irish golf development back then and only Eddie Hackett and myself seemed to get much work with him getting the lion's share.

Things needed stimulating and in the early-1980s, not knowing that a great golf boom was about to happen worldwide including in Ireland, I formed my first partnership with the legendary Henry Cotton who was a three-times winner of the British Open. He was easy to work with and having come through the hard times of World War II could teach you a thing or two about the value of money. When circumstances suggested it, I knew that he would agree to bringing Tom Craddock on-board as a third partner.

It was about 1986 when the first big design job in years arose on the Irish scene. Malahide Golf Club in Dublin was moving from its lovely old course in the town, making way for a housing project, and planning a 27-hole replacement close to Portmarnock. I decided to pitch for the job and my first move was to call the club's most famous member and my friend and hero- Tom Craddock!

Tom and I had been friends for decades. I had written about his genius in the early issues of Golf World in an effort to draw the attention of the R&A selectors to this Irish artisan golfer who was worthy of Walker Cup recognition. He helped a lot, of course, by being a winner of both the Irish Amateur Close and Irish Amateur Open titles as well as three East of Ireland titles. Irish golfers celebrated when he was picked for the 1967 Walker Cup team and retained his place in 1969.

Tom was a gentle, self-effacing fellow throughout and I was one of those who cherished his generous invitations to play practice rounds with him at various championships. He was an inspiration to us all, too, through his open loving relationship with his wife Nola and their shared love for their son Christopher.

So I had no hesitation in calling him for information on who-was-who within Malahide Golf Club and I thought that Christmas had come early when he told me that he was at that very moment the club president! Better still he said that he had often thought about getting into golf course design. I invited him to join me as a partner subject to the agreement of Henry Cotton.

I telephoned Henry and presented the case: Would you like to have one-third of the Malahide project or, as we stood,

Glashedy's ninth hole finds its way to the clubhouse.

the half of nothing? The answer was predictable and next day I had Tom and Nola on a plane to London to shake hands with the great man. Everything I ever did in golf was on the basis of a handshake. I never had a written contract in over thirty design projects and I was disappointed only once.

I prepared a big presentation of plans for Malahide, complete with aerial photography and detailed studies, and went along to present our case only to find that I was home alone when Tom telephoned me to say he was too ill to attend. So I was alone amongst strangers and we didn't get the job. But we had a grand new partnership which I decided to call Cotton, Craddock & Ruddy as the names were in alphabetical order, it listed us in descending age order and, of course, descending order in achievement as golfers. We didn't get to do any work together as a threesome because Henry died on December 22, 1987 at age 80.

Tom and I sparked into life building courses at the Ballymascanlon House Hotel in Dundalk, at St. Margaret's in Dublin, at Connemara Isles in Galway, at Druids Glen in Wicklow, at Ballyliffin in Donegal and extensions to courses at Wicklow and Killeen golf clubs. Neither Tom nor Henry had anything to do with The European Club which I guarded jealously as my own baby having bought the land, planned the links, developed the links and it was there that I was intent on spending the rest of my golf life.

After Ballyliffin and Druids we just drifted apart. Just as we had no written partnership we had no written parting. No bad words. Nothing but goodwill all around as before. After a while I heard that he had partnered with Eddie Hackett, who was getting old by then, and he then went solo at Claremoris in Mayo after Eddie's death at age 86 on December 16 in 1996.

My own solo path moved me to Portsalon, Rosapenna, Donegal, Montreal Island, Druids Heath and others and back to Ballyliffin for ongoing supervisions and revisions after Tom's death at age 67 on November 15, 1998. I visited him in hospital on the evening he died and it was just as ever before. Friends.

A shared passion for everything in golf, a shared interest in and trusting attitude towards other people, and a shared fondness for a mixed grill and ice-cream bonded Tom Craddock and myself! Sometimes we split-up and took turns going to Ballyliffin, he with Nola for company and I would bring Berndardine, on alternate weeks so that the free man could look-in at other jobs. When there together we would be out with the crew at 7a.m. and stay after them to plan the next day's work. We would huddle over every tilt within a green and confer over every bunker and every mound. With decisions made we would split-up and manage a team of workers each to direct every detail. We took care to be back to the Strand Hotel for dinner.

Brian Harkin was the man in the hotel then and his evening meals were magnificent. Huge mixed grills, washed down with a couple of pints of milk, neither Tom nor I ever touched alcohol, and a banana split! Heaven! Very often when the hotel was busy we shared a twin room and talked golf until sleep took us. Never, ever, in that time did I hear a bad word about anyone from Tom. He was a special, almost saintly man and I was lucky to know him.

The par-4 tenth on Glashedy covers gently heaving ground.

THE NEW ERA OF PLENTY
The new clubhouse and Nick Faldo came as surprises.

As work on the Glashedy Links came towards completion in 1995 the club sought to slow down spending. Or so we were told as we moved work along over the last few months.

We understood. We were, after all, playing a part in a miracle in the creation of a great second links in a tiny village where golf had been kept alive over the years on the basis of volunteer work and fund raising and had found itself on a sound financial footing only in the past decade or so.

Club treasurer Packie Farren had replaced Barry Kearney as the primary applier of pressure. "That's great," he would say as he admired the latest dramatic elements on the new links, "you are delivering the great links you promised. It is better even than The European Club," he would chuckle with a devilish smile, "but you will have to be aware that we do not have much money. We will have to be careful and get it done. We will have to stop spending soon."

We believed him. We were not wasting any time or any money in any case but we felt the urgent need to respond to the urgings of this most pleasant man whose affection and ambition for his community was palpable. So imagine our surprise when word came that the club was planning a new clubhouse. A vast new clubhouse at a cost approaching €1-million which was a pile of money back then!

"You have no money for a few bunkers," I whined in mock dismay, "but you are going to spend a €1-million building a pub! What sort of golfer are you?" We enjoyed the banter and shared the vision.

Of course, the entire club was on the move mentally by now. The Old Links was in superb condition and more popular than ever. The international publicity surrounding the Glashedy Links project was all positive and increasing volumes of visitors were coming to see what was happening.

The name Ballyliffin was into the world atlas of golf, into the worldwide dialogue about the best places to play, and there was talk of a couple of new hotels being planned in the village. It was felt, and it has proven to be so, that a great new golf resort was nearing the final stages of completion. An Irish version of St. Andrews or Pebble Beach and a venue to stand worthily alongside famous golf holiday venues like Ballybunion, Lahinch and Portrush.

Joe Findlay was an important part of the team at that time. He had been brought from Royal Portrush as the links manager and his dedication to detail was awesome during the vital growing-in period. Hour after hour he pounded away with his nail-board on the verges of greens and fairways preparing receptive beds for hand seeded grasses.

The par-4 eleventh on Glashedy approaches the big dune.

Such dedication to minute detail is the stuff that is required when seeking to bring a golf course into play in good order and without the "accidents" which can happen when lawnmowers are set too low too soon and move too fast on tender new grasses and bald patches begin to appear. Good greenkeeping is vital in the production of a golf course. It was an interesting moment when Joe announced that he was returning to Portrush as links manager. What would happen with the king of fescue gone away to his native place? As it happened, the Ballyliffin men produced a perfect answer in the person of Andy Robertson from Scotland. But more of him anon.

NICK FALDO SEEKS TO BUY BALLYLIFFIN

It was almost a surprise a minute in those days. We were just over a month into building The Glashedy Links when a helicopter arrived carrying Nick Faldo! What a surprise when we heard of this visit which happened on a day that we were back in Dublin! Nobody told us of the pending visit which, however, did a great deal of good for the club's reputation as Faldo put on record his view that the Old Links was "the most natural links he had ever played".

The next big news, indeed it was a bit of a shock, was that Nick Faldo's love for Ballyliffin had grown to such an extent that he wished to buy it! In 1996, within a year of the opening of the Glashedy Links to international acclaim, he made a bid for the club with its two links. A bold move by a man who had never backed off a shot during his illustrious playing career and now seemed intent on performing equally well in business.

The bid came at a time that the club was making a major effort financially and it must have seemed attractive to some to get out of debt so fast. But others felt that it would be wrong for the club to sell at all but especially at such a low price. It would be sad to sell after so many years of volunteerism and community work had delivered them so recently into the upper echelons of international golf. Besides, it appeared more of an opportunistic than a flattering offer as such an idea of a takeover, or such figures, would hardly be floated to Portrush or Portmarnock! After a long debate leading to an extraordinary general meeting the members voted against a sale.

That didn't end the Faldo connection with Ballyliffin. Friendship persisted and grew and eventually, in 2004, the club engaged the Nick Faldo golf design company to revise the bunkering on the Old Links. This came as a bolt from the blue to me as I had been allowing the club to get itself settled in its finances before resurrecting the original question posed to us twelve years earlier: Can you help revise bunkering on the Old Links?

I have never had a written contract with anyone but I believed that we had a clear understanding in the matter. We had suggested deferring the proposed bunkering project while a new links would be built. We had done the club good service. Exceptional service. So it was a shock that the bunkering of the Old Links had gone elsewhere.

Of course, the attachment of the Faldo name to the Old Links has been of marketing benefit to the club. The Old Links which has been shaped and moulded by Eddie Hackett, Charles Lawrie, Frank Pennink, Martin Hopkins, Tom Craddock, Pat Ruddy and Nick Faldo is a superb golf links which at once challenges and richly rewards the player.

The twelfth green on the Glashedy Links features lovely run-offs.

THE GOLDEN TRIANGLE
Glashedy's magical corner is extra special.

All the better golf courses have one or two truly outstanding sections which thrill the players and provide great fodder for dinner talk or day dreaming.

Amen Corner in Augusta with Rae's Creek wreaking havoc. The Road Hole at St. Andrews with the infamous Road Bunker. The ninth at Newcastle with the mountain backdrop. The island green at the seventeenth hole at Sawgrass. The lovely downhill drives at the eleventh at Ballybunion and the tenth at Rosses Point. The oceanside walks at the eighteenth at Pebble Beach and next door at the sixteenth at Cypress Point. The list goes on. Those who have been there cherish the memory. Those who have seen them in photographs long to go there.

At home at The European Club, when the golfers have gone home with a few hours of daylight left on a Summer's evening, I love to potter about with a few balls on the twelfth and thirteenth holes down by the beach. If I am at home in Glenageary it is the valley holes at Druids Glen, halfway between my home and The European Club, which beckon for a little twilight amusement.

There is something mystical about being out on a lovely landscape all alone as the sun declines and sends soft shadows flowing softly and stealthily into every hollow and behind every bush and tussock of grass taking extreme care not to ignore any opportunity to usher in another night. One rushes to get a few more good drives away before the sun sinks behind the hills, or into the ocean, and it is a bit disappointing when a heavy cloud spoils the moment by pulling its dark cloak over the orb and forcing a premature end.

Maybe one will get lucky and see a fox emerge, slowly and relaxed, to contemplate its early moves for a night which promises fine and plentiful dining. The unsuspecting rabbits bask in the sunset just behind a dune. Luxuriating in the lovely moment outside their burrows and never thinking that they may not be going home tonight. Life is like that. Golf is like that.

Ballyliffin is blessed with a multiplicity of magical corners but my number one choice is what I call the Golden Triangle formed by holes twelve, thirteen, fourteen and fifteen on Glashedy Links. I could continue playing a ball around those four holes forever and never get bored as my results would vary so and the light and wind and the very mood of the place would change endlessly but never fail to enchant.

I have hastened out to that place on many mornings in the pretext of looking at the progress being made with a new

The par-5 thirteenth is one of Glashedy's most famed holes.

bunker or with a new tee. Sometimes it has been frosty. As one scuttles up the hill to the twelfth tee one can be out of breath and just a little concerned that one has got here in time to have it all to oneself for a little while. There can be a dew on the ground and one hopes it will be sometime before somebody finds and follows one's footprints. It would be so nice to have it to oneself for a little time. Hopefully the greenkeepers will have made a slow start and do not come whirring up from the eleventh green too soon. It is so difficult to maintain a facade of kindness and civility when facing a person who has intruded on glorious solitude.

It is even better in the evening no matter what the weather. Sitting in the grass behind the green at the thirteenth, sheltered from the wind, allows one to imagine onself as an ancient Irish King sitting on his throne, formed by hills on three sides to provide the back and the arms to the throne, looking out over his lands and ocean and to Glashedy Rock standing proud in the waves.

Those men saw it all. The ocean whipped into a frenzy by ship guzzling storms. The waters of Pollan Bay twinkling placid and blue. The sloping sun prodding a rainbow into the sky. A scurrying rain cloud rushing along to shroud the mountains from view. Perhaps a ghoulish mist filling every depression with cotton wool! Sadly, too many golfers are consumed by par and bogey to take the time to dwell a little, to linger longer and savour the moment.

Sitting there in the grass the mind can wander around in the history of the Inishowen Peninsula which is the largest of the many great peninsulas around the Irish coastline and it boasts Ireland's most northerly point just a few miles away at Malin Head.

PLAYING A PART IN THE MAKING OF HISTORY

The golfers have played a brave part in the modern history of this place and it is easy to imagine their forebears giving smiles of approval if only they could see what has been happening in recent decades. Maybe they would be hopping mad if they realised what they are missing because many of them were feisty folk.

Inishowen, the island of Owen, is named in memory of Owen O'Neill who was a son of Niall of the Nine Hostages who in turn was a descendant of Conn of the Hundred Battles! Niall got his name from his method of rulership which was based substantially on the charming practice of holding hostage a member of the family of each sub-king or potentially troublesome neighbour.

Niall is of great interest to many golfers, including American-Irish golfers, today as he was a mighty warrior who was the Irish High King from about 375 to 400 A.D. and who enjoyed the finer things in life to the extent that a team of geneticists in Trinity College Dublin say it is possible that maybe three million men worldwide are his descendants. He still found time to play and his Y-chromosome DNA pattern M222 is found in about 20% of men in the northwest of Ireland and in about 2% of New Yorkers of European origin. It could be so when one considers the great number of Irish who have gone to America over the centuries and it is likely that a goodly number of visiting Irish-American golfers are getting closer to home than they realise when they swing into these parts.

Now, that is the kind of rambling that can go on in one's mind in the Golden Triangle at Ballyliffin. It isn't all about golf. It is about life and leisure and pleasure. But the golf is what brought us here and keeps drawing us back.

The holes in the Triangle don't form a triangle, really, but close enough to meet our purpose of lauding the landscape and golfing qualities of the place. They are arranged in a manner which brings the player from the twelfth tee through holes thirteen, fourteen and fifteen and back beside the twelfth tee again. In this way they present a mini-links of their own as one could keep playing around and around in this closed loop in the sure knowledge that golf doesn't have anything better or nicer to offer anywhere else.

They are perched on the plateau out at the far end of the links and afford magnificent views out over the dunes and over Pollan Bay and there in silent attendance is the ever present Glashedy Rock which has given the great new golf links its name.

A WIDE RANGE OF GOLF SHOTS

These four holes offer a wide range of golf shots and testing situations. The twelfth is a dog-leg to the right and it is balanced by the fifteenth which is a gentle dog-leg to the left. The thirteenth features a steep uphill approach to the green and the fourteenth comes teeming down that same hill on a parallel line.

The twelfth fairway offers a little shelter from the wind but there is no place to hide on the highest point on the links on the tee for the par-3 fourteenth where the full force of the wind comes into play on every inch of the body.

The greens are so varied. The twelfth features roll-offs to the back , the thirteenth is living treachery at the front and the fourteenth just loves to throw balls down the hill to the left.

The putting surfaces are individuals. The twelfth and the fifteenth are traditionalists with some strong rolls but some which are almost imperceptible to a poor eye. Try the eye on this: A A A A A A A A! Every one of those "A"s is important if it represents a pebble on your line or if you misread the putt by that much. Championships have been decided on such very fine margins. Spotting the smallest of those "A"s on your line from twenty paces can be difficult.

It is my thinking that anyone can detect a buried elephant but that it is so easy to miss a buried insect. The golfer with bad nerves and poor eyes, certainly with a strong cross-wind added, is fodder to the course designer. Which brings talk to the thirteenth green which has a few elephants buried in the back right corner and anyone trying to putt from there to the front left has to have the touch of a heart surgeon on a good day, or enough imagination to putt a sideways course to the target.

Add in a few other elements such as deep bunkers, steep slopes for the wayward golfer, uphill and downhill stances on the fairways and life is never dull in this place. It is possible to tune every shot in the bag on these four holes and to forget the cares of the world outside. It is over a mile to the sound of a motor vehicle and the planes bound for America are so high in the sky they are inaudible. So refreshing by comparison to those courses beside airports.

The fifteenth affords Glashedy's last view from the plateau.

A LINKS NEVER STOPS GROWING
As the game evolves the links must keep pace.

The task of designing and maintaining a golf links is never done. So much can go wrong if the attention wanders. A course can get dated and left out of the inner circle of fine golf if efforts are not made to keep pace with the evolution of the game.

Ongoing developments in the matter of the golf ball and equipment, the ever smoother playing surfaces, the popular war on rough grasses and deep bunkers, and the playing of the game by numbers with the aid of measuring devices need to be observed and evaluated if the golf course is to remain a pleasurable and meaningful challenge to sinew, nerve and brain in years to come.

Championship tests have stretched by over 1,000-yards in the past century. More than 25% of that has happened in the last thirty years and there is no end in sight as a new element comes into play with so many more people staying fit and young later into life. Millions of people today are athletes and are capable of stronger golf shots.

This is why I have always advised the owners of the golf courses I design that they should keep in touch in the years ahead and keep the situation under review. In some cases we are into a third decade of onward discussion but nowhere has it been taken to heart more than at Ballyliffin.

As recently as 2012-2013, all of seventeen years into the life of the Glashedy Links, we undertook a big programme to totally review the bunkering. As recently as Autumn 2013 we rebuilt the seventh green...not because there was anything wrong with it but it was thought that it could be better! Thinking and talking will continue thanks in no small part to one man, Patsy Doherty.

There is a great officer spirit within the club and many people serve long, quietly and steadfastly. Without them nothing could happen. But they are fortunate to have a man like Patsy Doherty, who was the club captain when the Glashedy project was first mooted in 1992, so intensely interested in the advancement of the two links in his role as greens convenor that he devotes many hundreds of hours per annum to the task.

Every club has, or should have, a greens convenor to dialogue with the officers and members on one side and work with the greenkeeping staff on the other. Few, if any, can hope to have a person as dedicated as Pastsy Doherty who will be found touring the links between 7a.m. and 8a.m. many mornings and again in the dusk. Looking at the grasses, at the bunkers, at the mowing patterns, the mowing quality and reviewing the machinery and the men.

Strong and varied bunkering on Glashedy's sixteenth fairway.

Rarely has one gone onto the links without seeing Patsy Doherty's red van bobbing along through the dunes. As often as not he is in conversation with links manager Andy Robertson who is the other vital cog in the equation.

It is important that a club should have a good head greensman. A man of knowledge who is capable of at once taking directions and delivering on them in a manner which achieves the goal expeditiously and economically while retaining the goodwill and good humour of the work force. Andy Robertson, a Scot, has done this flawlessly since he came to Ballyliffin from Sunningdale in 1998 and he and his entire team are a joy to work with and visit with. They care.

Which is important to the course designer who is akin to the gynaecologist who delivers a baby in good health and hands it over to the parents to rear. If the child is well cared for the result should be good. The same goes for a golf course. Sadly, if things are done badly and things go wrong, or a course is allowed to get shabby, the designer will often reap the whirlwind of criticism while the gynaecologist walks free even if a child he delivers becomes a murderer.

THE TEXAS WEDGE TELLS A STORY

The correct mowing of grasses for quality of cut and for pattern and location is very important. One of the ways to judge the quality of grass on a golf links is to see how it plays for those who are skilled with the Texas Wedge.

The putter has been known as the Texas Wedge ever since the early touring professionals in America found it wiser to run-up shots from the fringe with a putter stroke rather than attempting a swanky lofted chip when they found themselves playing off hardpan in pre-irrigation Texas! It was the percentage shot and it still works for those who know how.

One of these is a veteran Portmarnock member who showed great mastery of the art on a visit to The European Club. Crouched over the Texas Wedge on the twelfth, we were just pottering about and had started there to be near the sea, he was heard to mutter - "This is about the limit of my range" - as he swept a ball along the ground from eighty yards to within two steps of the flag. No divot. No effort. No risk. Just a vast amount of imagination with a sprinkling of intuition and skill. He repeated the performance at the very next hole, and again, and again.

How refreshing to watch as he stood in the midst of two-inch-deep divots, all of six-inches long, left by players in the groups ahead. Too many modern players see only the aerial route. Very few of them could have had such a good result digging with their shovels or whatever they use to do such damage to a fairway.

Ballyliffin is a superb place to bring your Texan. Most of the greens have a decent gap in front to allow for the running approach and Andy Robertson keeps his fescues so fine and groomed that it doesn't take an immense amount of hit to send a ground ball as much as one hundred yards. A wonderful shot to have in your arsenal when the winds blow as they really can in Donegal and anything that goes aloft can be an adventure.

Such fine surfaces present perfect conditions for wedge play as well, of course, so there is no question of confining the player to one type of shot. Rather, the menu of opportunity is on the table and a player can go to his strengths.

Big bunker on par-5 seventeenth fairway on Glashedy but not too deep.

Meanwhile, the bunkers at Ballyliffin, on both links, are of the highest standard in all respects … appearance, location, quality of sand, excellent drainage, gathering power, aesthetics and ability to intimidate. This is the result of several years of observation and revision.

It may seem strange to use the word "building" when referring to the making of bunkers. After all, they are just holes in the ground. Are they not? Maybe they were when they were created by sheep digging holes in the sand to shelter from the wind. But nowadays a bunker is a work of art and, in the minds of some, the work of the devil.

If a bunker is to be of any use other than merely decorative it has to be a bit of a nuisance. As often as not the good bunker will come under attack from the club committee who want to have it back-filled! If it is not in play at all one must ask why it should be there at all.

THE SKILL OF BUNKER BUILDING

A full audit of Ballyliffin Glashedy's bunkers was undertaken in 2012 to measure them against the modern player and for resistance to wind blow, as loose sand is an easy victim to high winds in these parts, and for ease of maintenance. The decision was made to revet the faces throughout, that is to give them stacked grass-sod walls, in a new way with soft entrances just graded into gentle "walkinable" shapes. A total 360-degree revetted wall can present a harsh and artificial look as well as gobbling-up acres of sod and requiring the same volumes again at restoration times.

Andy Robertson's skills at revetting made the job seem easy and he was generous in passing his knowledge to his staff all of whom responded enthusiastically and enjoyed seeing the varied bunkers take shape. There was no complaint even when I asked for extra difficult curves to be created. We were artists pursuing a brilliant outcome.

Great efforts were made to vary the shapes of the bunkers, not all that usual on a links, with both the vertical and the horizontal lines moving in sometimes strong and sometimes gentle curves. All the time taking care to ensure that the highest faces were directly in line with the direction of play most likely to be chosen by the escaping prisoner (sorry, I mean the escaping golfer). This latter point is most important as it is a frequent mistake to place the higher lips where they look best rather than where they are needed to add challenge and interest to the game.

Great care was taken to select or to create surrounds which would make the high lips look great and natural. To grade the bunkers into the surrounding land features. To make it look as though natural sites presented themselves at just the correct location for drives and approach shots of varying lengths! Nature was never so kind. A bunker requires building into the terrain just as carefully as a green does.

The modern golfer comes in so many shapes and sizes that it is impossible to place one fairway bunker to suit all. So it is that in many cases two or three bunkers have been set to work together presenting variations of distance and line. The greenside bunkers are for all-comers.

The work will continue at Glashedy. Those who have shared the joys of its birth will guard it jealously and joyfully.

The last hole on Glashedy presents a challenging dog leg. The drive needs to be strong and true to gain a view of the green.

LOVE AFFAIR WITH DONEGAL
And with championship golf ....

Looking back over forty years of working at golf course design a few patterns emerge. It becomes clear that I have had the privilige of creating a great many links holes and that the courses I have built attract championship play with eight of my courses having hosted a total of twenty-five championships to date and with two more events scheduled. They say that a golf course should have the ability to identify the best player as champion and if this is true I am very happy that the list of winners at my venues includes Rory McIlroy, Padraig Harrington, Colin Montgomerie, Sergio Garcia and the great champion ladies Laura Davies and Sophie Gustafson.

While links golf has dominated a lot of my golf design life I have been thrilled with the outcome of many of my inland works, too, and not least the two courses at Druids Glen and the two courses at Montreal Island.

The European Club, my own pet in Wicklow, was my first major foray into links design. It was quickly followed by the commission to work with my late design partner and friend Tom Craddock in designing the Ballyliffin Glashedy links and introducing a number of new holes on the old links there.

It was back solo as a designer then for a quite remarkable run of links design in County Donegal as I introduced eleven new holes to transform Portsalon from a lovely old style local links into a modern beauty, redesigned eight holes at Donegal (with further works pending there in 2015) and created Sandy Hills Links and a new-nine on the Old Tom Morris links at Rosapenna. No wonder I love County Donegal and I am delighted that the county is now one of the greatest centres of high quality golf in the world.

Of course, the playing of championships on one's designs is the surest way to test the quality of the workmanship. This came to a climax in 2007 and 2008 when we hosted the Irish Professional Championship at The European Club in the week preceding the British Open both years. The objective was to prepare Padraig Harrington for the Open and it worked sensationally well as I set-up the links as close as possible to Open quality in 2007, with high rough and dynamite fast greens, and Harrington won in a playoff before going to Carnoustie and winning The Open in a playoff the next weekend. It had been a perfect dress rehearsal.

In 2008, I sought to set-up the links as close as possible to what would be found at the Open at Birkdale the following week. What a thrill it was when Harrington won by four with us and then retained his Open crown at Birkdale by the same margin. It was no coincidence that the winning score at the Open was four strokes fewer than the winning score at The European Club both years. We had hit the precise winning design formula for the biggest event in golf.

Flowers in the rough on Glashedy's eighteenth hole.

CHAMPIONSHIPS PLAYED ON GOLF COURSES DESIGNED BY PAT RUDDY

1994-	Irish Ladies' Open Championship at St. Margaret's	Laura Davies
1996-	Murphys Irish Open Championship at Druids Glen	Colin Montgomerie
1997-	Murphys Irish Open Championship at Druids Glen	Colin Montgomerie
1997-	AIB Irish Seniors' Open Championship at St. Margaret's	Tommy Horton
1998-	Murphys Irish Open Championship at Druids Glen	David Carter
1998-	Irish Ladies' Open Championship at Ballyliffin	Sophie Gustafson
1999-	Murphys Irish Open Championship at Druids Glen	Sergio Garcia
2001-	Irish Ladies' Amateur Close Championship at The European Club	Alison Coffey
2002-	Northwest Ireland Professional Open at Ballyliffin	Adam Mednick
2002-	Severiano Ballesteros Trophy at Druids Glen	GB&I beat Europe
2003-	Irish Ladies' Amateur Close Championship at Donegal	Martina Gillen
2004-	Irish Men's Amateur Close Championship at Donegal	Brian McElhinney
2004-	Irish Professional Close Championship at St. Margaret's	Padraig Harrington
2004-	Montreal Open Professional Championship at Montreal Island	Stephen Woodard
2005-	Irish Ladies' Amateur Close Championship at Portsalon	Patricia Mangan
2005-	Montreal Open Professional Championship at Montreal Island	Peter Tomasulo
2006-	Irish Professional Close Championship at Druids Heath	David Mortimer
2006-	Irish Ladies' Amateur Close Championship at The European Club	Patricia Mangan
2006-	Irish Men's Amateur Close Championship at The European Club	Rory McIlroy
2007-	Leinster Youths' Open Championship at The European Club	Dara Lernihan
2007-	Irish Professional Close Championship at The European Club	Padraig Harrington
2008-	Irish Professional Close Championship at The European Club	Padraig Harrington
2009-	Irish Professional Close Championship at The European Club	Padraig Harrington
2013-	Leinster Youths' Open Championship at The European Club	Gary Collins
2013-	Carey Cup - Irish Amateurs v Metropolitan NY at The European Club	Metropolitan NY win
2016-	Irish Men's Amateur Close Championship at Ballyliffin Glashedy	
2018-	Irish Men's Amateur Close Championship at The European Club	

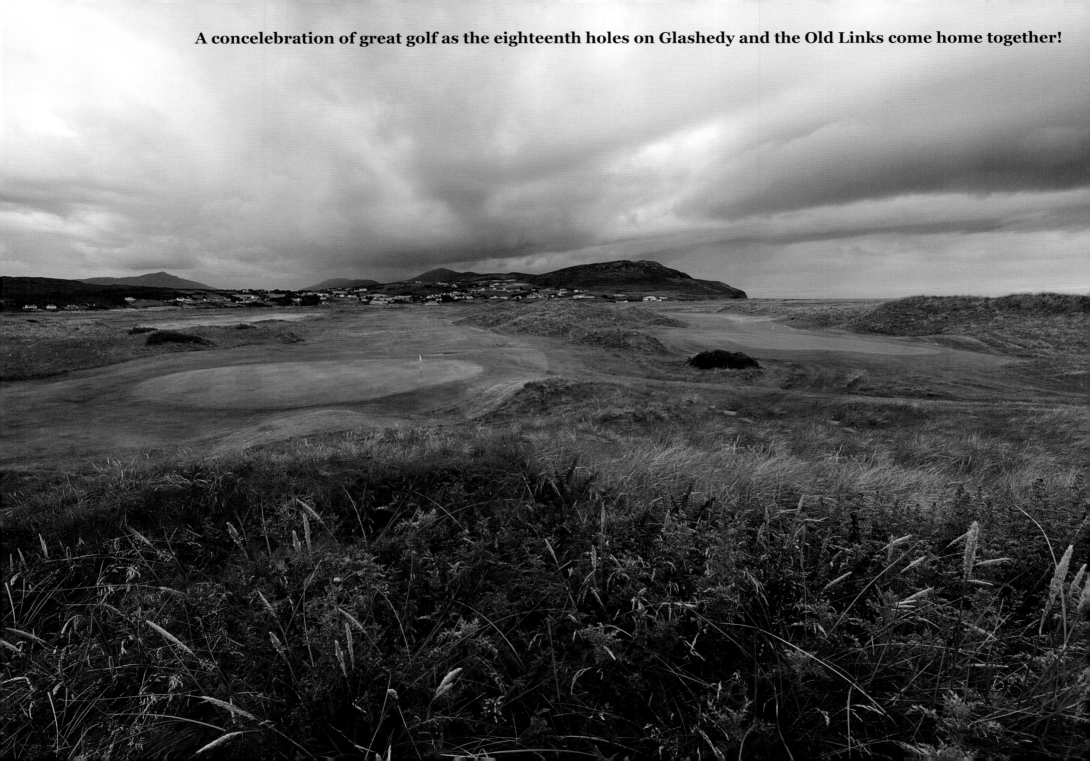

A concelebration of great golf as the eighteenth holes on Glashedy and the Old Links come home together!

Looking Good From All Sides

Ballyliffin is one of those rare golf places that looks beautiful no matter whether looked at forward, back or sideways.
The rippling fairways on the Old Links greet one right away on holes one and ten as seen in the top picture.
The new thirteenth hole created by Tom Craddock and Pat Ruddy plays superbly and brings the player to the end of a valley furthest from home and from which the view back to the clubhouse and mountains is breathtaking, above.
It is hoped the golfers of Ballyliffin, will share happy times in this remarkable place for centuries to come.
Good luck, folks, and swing away ...... I will see you along the fairway, Pat Ruddy.